Y0-BSE-204

winelands of the cape

winelands of the cape

PHOTOGRAPHED BY CHRIS JANSEN

Published by Don Nelson
Cape Town 1980

First edition 1980
Text Maureen Joubert

ISBN 0 909238 48 0
Designed by Peter Ibbotson
Lithographic reproduction by Hirt & Carter (Pty) Ltd., Cape Town
Printed by Printpak (Cape) Ltd., Cape Town

Long life to the grape! for when summer is flown
The age of our nectar shall gladden our own.

Byron, from *Fill the Goblet Again*

INTRODUCTION

The mere mention of this country's wine-producing areas conjures up images of the beautiful Upper Berg River Valley, historic homesteads, the towering mountains surrounding Van der Stel's village, and lush vineyard-carpeted countryside flanking the Breede River. These are the well-trodden paths of our winelands. But vines flourish and wine is made in areas beyond these: along the Olifants River, on the wide stretches atop the Cedarberg, along the Lower Orange River region and in the Swartland district, and also in places with names too seldom connected with wine: Lutzville, Trawal, Calitzdorp, Vaalharts, Keimoes, Grootdrink, Oudtshoorn and De Rust.

In 1656 Jan van Riebeeck planted the first vines in the Dutch East India Company Garden beneath Table Mountain, and in 1659 he was able to write in his diary:

"Today, praise be to the Lord, wine was made for the first time from Cape grapes."

It was Governor Simon van der Stel who really pioneered wine-making at the Cape, establishing a homestead and flourishing wine-farm in the Constantia valley, and encouraging exploration and expansion into the interior, as a result of which Stellenbosch was founded on the banks of the Eerste River in 1679. This fertile area soon showed its potential for viticulture and thus the tradition of Stellenbosch wine-making began.

In 1688 the Huguenots, religious refugees from France, settled in the Groot Drakenstein area, and their technical expertise was an invaluable contribution to the young wine industry.

During the Napoleonic Wars, when French wine was unobtainable, Britain offered preferential tariffs on Cape wines, which greatly encouraged production, but in 1861 this was abolished and South African exports dwindled.

Another major setback took place in 1885 when Cape vineyards were ravaged by *Phylloxera,* a virulent disease. New vine shoots had to be grafted onto disease-resistant American rootstock.

The history of wine-making at the Cape had its beginnings at the outset of our country's development, yet it remains a babe in arms when compared to the industry in wine-growing countries in Europe, and even more so when authorities trace the history of the vine back 8 000 years. On the other hand it gives one a warm sense of achievement when comparisons are made. Thanks to suitable soils, the necessary variations, equable climate, modern equipment and technique and, above all, a band of dedicated and knowledgeable wine-makers, South African wines have been acclaimed excellent quality for money by the most discerning connoisseurs.

We are able to produce a wide variety of high quality brandies, port wines, South African sherries and a broad spectrum of table wines. There are wines with individuality to please the palate of every wine-drinker: sweet and heady dessert wines, fruity semi-sweets and late harvests, crisp, clear and dry whites, light reds and round, lingering and full-bodied reds.

This variety and quality can partly be seen as the result of the awakening to table wines in the sixties. Consumer needs encouraged producers to compete and improve their products. Today the industry is vital, expanding, experimenting and broadening its activities.

As the history of wine-making in South Africa developed, individuality in character became noticeable. Names of farms, areas and cultivars were coupled with products with a distinct character which gave pleasure to the serious wine-lover. It was only in 1972, however, that legal definition and recognition was granted to wines of particular areas, as well as wine produced from specific cultivars and vintages.

This "Wines of Origin" Legislation took into consideration factors such as the influence of the soil, location and climatic conditions, along with the skills and techniques of viticultural practitioners. Nature, however, was given first priority. This legislation brought about a tremendous change in the pattern of wine-making, but is basically a simple system. Production units are demarcated as defined areas whose boundaries are determined by law. The smallest units, the estates, are grouped into wards which are further grouped into districts. The districts are grouped into regions, the largest unit.

The winelands can be visited at any time of the year, each season bringing its own charm. The visitor needs a good map and a clear idea of his particular interests regarding wine, architecture and/or landscape, but please simplify matters by checking the times of tours and sales beforehand, since these often change with the seasons or the priorities of the wine-maker. Since there are 53 demarcated estates in the winelands and some 73 co-operative cellars, it will be attempting the impossible to mention every one. We are therefore giving preference to places included on the established wine routes with further mention of well-known names.

CAPE PENINSULA

From Cape Town the traveller can reach several sections of the winelands, but it would be foolhardy to attempt too many stops within one day. A visit to **Groot Constantia** will in all probability top the list, since no wine-lover on a visit to the Cape can afford to bypass this historic cradle of the South African wine industry.

In spite of encroaching development in the area, the land that once belonged to Simon van der Stel is jealously protected and the estate includes five historic homesteads: Groot Constantia, Nova Constantia, de Hoop op Constantia, Klein Constantia and Buitenverwachting. State-owned and managed by the Oenological and Viticultural Research Institute, the accent here is on quality red wines. The vineyards are located on red soil of granatic origin, while warm dry summers and proximity to the sea make the district particularly suited to the production of these wines. The first names that spring to mind are those of cabernet sauvignon, shiraz and pinotage with pinot noir and white varieties gaining more recognition. Modern techniques used in wine-making here promise a great future for the estate.

Groot Constantia also recalls the past, the glorious days of wine made by J.P. Cloete at the turn of the 18th century. Enjoyed by the nobility of Europe, sought after by Napoleon, Louis XVI and even Bismarck, amongst others, the wine was immortalised in the writings of famous visitors to the Cape such as Jane Austen, Baudelaire, Alexandre Dumas and Anthony Trollope. Another relic of a glorious past is the Cape Dutch homestead, Groot Constantia, exquisitely restored and furnished with antique pieces. Wine is sold at the cellar and lunches are served on the estate.

The only other wine district within the Cape Divisional Council area is Durbanville. Here the vineyards are unexpectedly encountered on the slopes of Tygerberg, 15 km from the sea and within a stone's throw of the city of Bellville. Only two estates have survived the encroachment by the expanding metropolitan area: **Meerendal** (where the Starke family have been making exceptionally good wines since 1934) and **Diemersdal**. The area is particularly suited for the production of pinotage, cabernet sauvignon and shiraz.

The best way to reach the winelands is by car, as the estates are spread over large areas and a car enables one to select and explore areas of particular interest. The national road (N1) out of Cape Town takes one to Paarl, and a turn-off before Paarl itself takes one eastwards to Stellenbosch on the R304.

Stellenbosch can also be reached from the eastern side, by taking the national road (N2) out of Cape Town towards Somerset West and then turning off onto the R310.

Several organised bus tours are also available. Springbok Atlas Safaris have half-day tours which

Engraving of Groot Constantia in 1741. The legend indicates the "vineyard wherein grows the highly-thought-of Constantia wine."
(Cape Archives)

visit only one estate, and one-day sight-seeing tours to Paarl, Franschhoek and Stellenbosch. Satour have a one-day tour visiting three wineries and also a one-day tour to Paarl, the KWV and one Stellenbosch estate. Fairest Cape Tours, based in Somerset West, run two flexible tours of the winelands, full or half day, accommodating not more than nine people and visiting as many estates and places of interest as possible.

There are daily trains from Cape Town to Stellenbosch, Paarl and Somerset West, and cars may be hired in these towns.

STELLENBOSCH

Going further afield, travellers will probably want to visit Stellenbosch. Little wonder, for Stellenbosch has much to offer the tourist: a tradition of more than three centuries that has brought it fame as a cultural and educational centre, an example of modern-day restoration and conservation of an architectural heritage and also as a wine-producing area. It was here that the first wine route was introduced in 1971. The brainchild of two of the district's best-known wine-farmers, Frans Malan (Simonsig) and Niel Joubert (Spier) and with the enthusiastic support of Spatz Sperling (Delheim), it has grown into a tremendous tourist attraction and instigated a better understanding of wines and increased sales. At twelve private cellars and four co-operative cellars along the route more than 100 wines can be tasted and bought. There is also the opportunity to explore the process of wine-making and often the chance to share views with the winemaker over a glass of wine. A map of the route is available from the offices of the Stellenbosch Wine Route at Doornbosch, Strand Street, P.O. Box 204, Stellenbosch. (Tel: 02231-4310) and as a guide we are mentioning stops as they appear along the four major roads leading to Stellenbosch.

The wine route emblem, three castles on a red and yellow shield, surmounted by a plumed helmet, is used to indicate the sections of the wine route, and several of the estates have notices at their gates indicating when they are open to the public.

The first group of estates can easily be reached when branching off from the national road (N2) between Cape Town and Somerset West on the R310. Before reaching the first wine route stop on this road, one passes two of the area's most prestigious estates, **Vergenoegd** and **Meerlust.** Apart from producing superb red wines, both estates have impressive manor houses.

At **Vergenoegd** the homestead gable bears the date 1773, but was probably added a few decades after the original building was erected. The Faures have owned the farm since 1820 and it was here that "flor" yeast was found by Dr C. Niehaus, South Africa's 'father' of sherry.

The neighbouring **Meerlust** estate has one of the most frequently photographed manor houses, with a striking gable and thatched roof. The rich, loamy soil and cool sea breeze combine with the fine technology practised here to produce truly great red wines. The estate is not open to the public.

A stop at **Spier** estate is well worthwhile. Granted to Arnout Janz in 1692 and named after his home town, Speyer, in Germany, a remarkable complex of historic buildings is grouped together. These have been carefully restored by the present owner, Mr Niel Joubert, whose son Chris assists him on the estate, which also includes the farm Goedgeloof. Wines can be bought and sampled in the attractive wine-cellars and meals are served in the restaurant. The Jonkershuis Wine House offers light lunches which can also be enjoyed under the oaks. Tel: 02234-468, 232 (wine sales and general), 242 (restaurant), 512 (Jonkershuis Wine House).

Two co-operative cellars on the wine route are situated nearby: Vlottenburg and Eersterivier-vallei. Both produce award-winning wines and offer a warm welcome to visitors. Modern cellar techniques and cold fermentation ensure excellent white wines, while reds are also available. Vlottenburg: Tel: 02234-493. Eersterivier-Vallei: Tel: 02234-477.

From here a short drive brings the traveller to **Uiterwyk** estate, situated in the Stellenbosch Valley. The road meanders through the panoramic valley and leads to the entrance of the Cape Dutch homestead of the De Waals, built in 1791 and declared a national monument in 1975. Danie de Waal and his son Chris are responsible for the excellent wines made in the modern cellar which started operating in 1979. The old cellar

Coat of Arms of Stellenbosch. (Cape Archives)

was built in 1795 and continuously used for 180 years. Tel: 02231-2788.

Situated on the same route is another family concern, **Overgaauw** estate, owned and run by David van Velden and his son Braam. The first grapes were pressed at Overgaauw in 1909 by Abraham van Velden and today this tradition is carried on with the production of white and red wines. Only the best wines are selected for bottling on the estate. Tel: 02234-265.

Driving towards Stellenbosch one can visit **Neethlingshof** estate, and once more admire the craftmanship of builders of the past. The manor house, built in 1814, has been declared a national monument and preserved with care by the present owner, Jannie Momberg. A modern fermentation cellar and tasting room were added in 1978. A wide range of red and white wines is produced on the farm and sold to the public. Tel: 02231-2889, 71472.

The neighbouring estate, **Verdun,** is owned by Kosie Roux, representing the fifth generation to proceed in the tradition as a wine-farmer on this farm. White and red dry wines are made in the cellar which has a section dating back to 1795. Tel: 02231-5227.

Just before entering Stellenbosch there is a turnoff to the left which takes one through the beautiful Devon Valley to the **Devon Valley** estate and further to **Montagne.** Wines are not sold on these estates, but can be obtained from most bottle-stores (Wines produced at Devon Valley are sold under the Bertrams label).

Devon Valley offers the visitor an informative tour through the modern white wine cellar and classical red wine maturation cellars. The surrounding site is open to visitors for picnics and braais. Tel: 02231-70300.

The history of **Montagne** can be traced to 1704 and the homestead was built in 1849. The original wine-cellar has been redesigned and equipped with modern winemaking machinery. Tel: 02232-245, 268.

From this point the historic town of Stellenbosch can be visited. Governor Simon van der Stel founded the town in 1679 and encouraged settlers to build homesteads and establish farms. He was also responsible for planting oak trees in the town, the descendents of which still line the streets and rivers of Stellenbosch, giving it the name *Eikestad* ("Oak City").

In the centre of the town is the *Braak,* a grassed common which was originally used as a parade ground. It is surrounded by buildings of historical interest, such as the *Kruithuis* (the old arsenal), which now houses a small military museum, the Rhenish Mission Church and the *Burgerhuis.* St Mary's Church is a tiny thatched church on the *Braak* itself.

Dorp Street has a series of perfectly restored old houses, in one of which (no. 149) is housed a collection of the works of Pierneef. There are several other churches and museums in this central area, including *Libertas Parva* (29 Dorp St), a restored homestead dating back to 1780, which houses the Rembrandt van Rijn Art Foundation. Nearby are the Stellenryck Wine Museum and the Distillers Brandy Museum, showpieces of the Oude Meester group.

Another facet of Stellenbosch is the University, which is the oldest Afrikaans university in South Africa. The campus with 10 000 students is situated near the centre of the town, and the residences are scattered throughout the town, so that during the university term the peace of the historic oak-lined streets is offset by the liveliness of the student population.

There are several restaurants specializing in traditional food, such as the Lanzerac Hotel, a restored farmstead on the Jonkershoek Road, De Volkskombuis and Doornbosch (A KWV winehouse) on the old Strand road, and De Kelder, a restaurant in the cellar of the old farm Vredelust.

Stellenbosch is also the home of several large liquor concerns whose names are known throughout the country.

STELLENBOSCH FARMERS' WINERY

The Stellenbosch Farmers' Winery was founded in 1924 by William Charles Winshaw to "give people good wine at a price they can afford." Thus apart from developing new wines in various price ranges, innovations such as larger, more economical wine containers have been introduced.

Stellenbosch Farmers' Winery products include the more expensive Zonnebloem and Oude Libertas ranges, as well as lower priced wines such as Zonnheimer and Kellerprinz.

The latest phase in the long-term plan to promote natural wines in South Africa is the establishment of Wine Centres in seven major cities of South Africa, staffed with Wine Advisers qualified to answer questions from the public about any aspect of wine.

The purpose of the publicity campaign is to foster public awareness of the availability, variety and quality of South African wines, which will help to improve the wine market, to the benefit of both producer and consumer.

OUDE MEESTER GROUP

When the Oude Meester Group took over Distillers Corporation, the group decided to build a new cellar for developing and marketing as wide a range as possible of high quality wines. Accordingly, the Bergkelder was built on the southern slopes of the Papegaaiberg near Stellenbosch, enabling the group's winemakers to have access to superb quality grapes from selected estates in the region, in return for which the estates receive expert advice on any aspect of production.

The Bergkelder continued to produce the wines taken over from the Distillers Corporation, and developed its own wines of top quality such as the "Fleur du Cap" range.

The Bergkelder also handles exclusively the marketing of the wines of several estates, such as Alto, Allesverloren, Bonfoi, De Wetshof, Goede Hoop, Hazendal, Jacobsdal, Koopmanskloof, Meerendal, Meerlust, Middelvlei, Theuniskraal, Uitkyk and Zandvliet.

Another interest of the Oude Meester group is the preservation of historic buildings. The group was involved in the restoration of De Oude Drostdy at Tulbagh, which was badly damaged in the earth tremors of 1969, and also has two museums attached to its headquarters in the centre of Stellenbosch, the Stellenryck Wine Museum with its well-known German wine press in the courtyard, and the Distillers Brandy Museum.

GILBEY'S

The name Gilbey has been associated with the South African wine trade since Walter and Alfred Gilbey pioneered the sale of Cape wines in Britain in 1857.

The company W. & A. Gilbey was founded in Pietermaritzburg in 1950, the first distillery to produce gin locally, and in 1962 took over the Cape wine and brandy company R. Santhagens, establishing a headquarters in De Oude Molen, a restored wheat mill in Stellenbosch dating back to 1710.

Gilbey-Santhagens soon had country-wide connections, with a distillery in Johannesburg and Stellenbosch, wine and brandy maturation cellars and their own wine farm, Klein Zalze.

In 1970 the name was changed to Gilbey's Distillers & Vintners, and in 1972 the company took over Bertrams Wines of Stellenbosch. Gilbey's is now the leading independent liquor producer in South Africa, as well as marketing the products of several privately owned estates such as Twee Jongegezellen, Alphen and Hartenberg.

As well as regular wine tours, Gilbey's runs a monthly three day seminar on wine at De Oude Molen, which can be attended by anyone interested.

Blaauwklippen estate is situated about 4 km from Stellenbosch on the R44. It has much to offer the visitor: good wine, an impressive collection of antiques and wagons, Cape kitchen products and cheeses made on the farm, cellar tours and the visual pleasure of traditional Cape Dutch architecture. During the tourist season the estate can be inspected by horse-drawn carriage and coachman's lunches are served under the oaks. Tel: 02231-71245, 71276.

Section 9 of the wine route leads to **Rust-en-Vrede,** the estate recently bought and restored by Jannie Engelbrecht. The existing cellar was built in 1790, and the homestead in 1825. Wine-making was resumed after many decades when the former rugby Springbok restored the cellar. Appointments necessary. Tel: 02234-436.

Another approach to Stellenbosch is from the national road between Cape Town and Paarl (N1), turning off at the Klipheuwel exit on the R304. Section no. 2 of the wine route takes one to **Simonsig** where the largest selection of varietal wines marketed by any wine-maker in South Africa is produced. The estate belongs to Frans Malan, an enthusiastic and go-ahead wine-maker and consists of the farms Simonsig and De Hoop. From this cellar came the first South African sparkling wine made by the *methodé champenoise*. Tel: 02232-304, 297, 398.

The Kromme Rhee Road reaches the Klapmuts Road and brings one to a valley with two impressive stops. It is the romance of unchanged wine-making that greets one at **Muratie**. The farm with its lovely homestead built in the 1800's was bought by the German artist Georg Canitz in 1925 and developed into a fine wine farm. Here the first pinot noir vineyards were planted in South Africa. In 1959 Canitz's daughter Annemarie took over the management of the farm and in Ben Prins she has a loyal and dedicated wine-maker. Wines are tasted in the rustic cellar in an atmosphere of wood and must and dust-crusted bottles. Tel: 02232- 330 and 336.

The road leads further to **Delheim** along the south-easterly slopes of Simonsberg. Delheim wines are produced on the farm Driesprongh and cover a large selection of varietals. Cheese lunches are offered in the tourist season and can be enjoyed on the stretch of lawn overlooking the valley towards Table Mountain. Tel: 02232-394, 434.

Two more co-operative cellars form part of the wine route and are worth a visit. They will be clearly marked on your wine route map: De Helderberg Co-op (Tel: 024-42476, 42403) and Bottelary Co-op (Tel: 02232-204).

Several estates are not on the Stellenbosch Wine Route. **Kanonkop-Kriekbult** is situated off the Klapmuts/Stellenbosch road. Since 1969 Jan "Boland" Coetzee has been in charge of wine-making here and has proven himself one of the very best. The wine for sale on the estate is limited and the demand enormous. Tel: 02233-417.

Schoongezicht/Rustenberg started out as Rustenberg in 1699, was later sub-divided and thus became two farms, the second named Schoongezicht. In 1945 Peter Barlow re-united the property. For many people the setting and style of this farm is the most beautiful in the winelands and always worth a visit. The wines produced here are equally popular. Reds are sold under the Rustenberg label, whites under the Schoongezicht one, but both come from the same cellar. Tel: 02231-71006.

Although not open to the general public, mention must be made of **Uitkyk.** The double-storeyed house, built in 1788, is a fine example of the architecture of Thibault and so unlike the Cape Dutch homesteads associated with many wine estates. The name Uitkyk will always be connected with a wine that is today still considered one of the best produced locally: Carlonet, a blend of cinsaut and cabernet sauvignon, first produced by Baron Von Carlowitz and his son George. The excellent wines from Uitkyk are today marketed through the Bergkelder. No wine is sold on the estate.

Audacia, on the slopes of the Helderberg, produces excellent red wines which are sold on the estate.

Alto can also be considered one of the great names in South Africa's wine history, especially where the Alto Rouge is concerned. These wines are now marketed through the Bergkelder and the estate is not open to the public.

At the **Vredenburg** estate along the Faure Road wine is sold under the Vredenheim label — while supplies last, so do check beforehand. The restored homestead with its impressive gable was built in 1789 and since 1926 the Neethling family has produced excellent wine products here, which at one time were exported directly to England and Germany. Tel: 02234-492.

PAARL

Following the success of the Stellenbosch Wine Route, the Paarl Wineway was opened in 1978. It offers the visitor the opportunity to meet the people and the wines of an area also steeped in history and tradition.

Here Huguenot and Dutch farmers settled in the late 17th century, the Afrikaans language movement originated and a cultural and architectural heritage is today still preserved. The area is centred around Paarl, which stretches along the Berg River and the foot of the mountain which gave it its name, Paarlberg (Pearl Mountain).

In this town many historical buildings, museums and the Afrikaans Language Monument can be visited, and a drive along the Jan Phillips Drive to the natural garden of indigenous flowers is an unforgettable experience.

Paarl itself makes an excellent starting point on the wineway. It is, after all, the home of KWV, the national co-operative of South African wine-producers. This organisation was established in 1918 and now controls wine production and promotes the interests of members locally and overseas.

The KWV cellars can be visited and wine tastings are included in these tours. The cellars cover about 15 hectares and have a storing capacity of some 1 400 000 hectolitres. Towards the mountain and within walking distance of KWV's impressive head office, **Laborie** estate is situated. The estate belongs to KWV and consists of a restored Cape Dutch manor house, a historical wine cellar where lectures and demonstrations and wine courses are held, a modern pressing cellar, a guest house and the Laborie wine house, where wines from the area are served with traditional dishes. Reservations should be made by 'phoning 0251-26320. Tel: 0251-22011 for information on cellar tours.

De Soete Inval estate is situated on the banks of the Berg River, just outside Paarl. Here Robert Frater, a Scottish immigrant, started a wool-washing business in 1869. His grandson planted the first vines and today red wines are still made by the family on the estate. Wines are not for sale on the property, but can be purchased at the Central Hotel on the Main Street of Paarl.

The road to Wellington takes one past **Nederburg,** the home of the annual auction of rare Cape wines, a premier event in the South African wine calendar, which attracts visitors from overseas countries such as Britain, America, West Germany and Argentina.

The farm was named by a German immigrant in 1792, and developed as one of our leading wine-producing farms by Johann Graue, who set the pace in the South African wine industry for technical innovation and meticulous observation and improvement of performance. These consistently high standards were maintained by the capable and talented wine-maker Gunther Brözel after Graue's retirement, and over the years have been responsible for wines which have won many internationally coveted awards.

Visits can be arranged by phoning 0251-22044.

By-passing Paarl on the Agter-Paarl Road, a number of respected estates can be reached. **Landskroon** estate is situated on the south-western slope of the mountain and has been inhabited since 1692. It became the property of the De Villiers family in 1872, and in the early forties Paul de Villiers, the grandson of the first De Villiers to farm at Landskroon, planted red cultivars for the making of port wines. Today splendid ports are still produced, but the wide variety of red cultivars has enabled Paul and Hugo de Villiers to produce one of the largest ranges of dry red estate-produced and bottled wines in the country. Tel: 0251-26406.

About 1 km further lies **Fairview** estates, owned by Cyril Back, brother of Sydney, whose estate **Backsberg** is further on this wineway. The farm has been in the Back family since 1937 and the first wines were bottled for sale under their own label in 1974. This entire bottling was sold on the first wine auction to be held on an estate in South Africa. Tel: 0251-5141.

Boschendal estate is beautifully situated in the Drakenstein Valley and well worth a visit. It has an impressive history and one of the country's best-known stately farmsteads, built in 1812. The manor house is open to the public and has been furnished with pieces dating back to the Dutch East India Company, and it also contains a remarkable collection of Kraak porcelain. Wine is made in a modern cellar and sold on the estate, while buffet lunches are served in a restored outbuilding, as well as dinner on Friday and Saturday evenings. Tel: 0251-4252 (restaurant) and 4281 (wine sales).

From Boschendal the road to Cape Town takes one to **Backsberg** estate, a name held in high esteem by wine-lovers. Sydney Back has turned the estate into a haven for the visitor with a sincere interest in wine. A closed circuit television system enables one to see how young vines are propagated, vineyards established and cared for, grapes harvested and wine made and bottled. After the cellar tour a visit can be made to the small museum with its early wine-making equipment and wines of the estate sampled. Tel: 0251-5141.

Wine-making and wildlife are combined at **Wiesenhof** near Backsberg. A drive through the estate takes one to the peak of the Skurweberg Ridge (600 m above sea level) where the observation tower gives a dramatic view of the Western Cape winelands, two oceans, mountain ranges, vineyards and the surrounding villages. Game roams the farmland and a boating lake offers idyllic recreation. Tel: 0251-5181.

For a continental touch, make your last stop **Villiera** estate, where light Austrian lunches are served in the tourist season. Run by two young Austrians, the estate initially produced wine for the Austrian market. The wines from Villiera are still shipped to Austria, but an enthusiastic following locally has created a further market in South Africa. Tel: 02232-383, 302.

This wineway also includes a number of co-operative wineries, many producing excellent wines, which are for sale. The following co-ops appear on the Wineway map:
Paarl-Vallei Co-operative;
The Wellington Co-operative; *
The Wamakersvallei Co-operative; *
Bovlei Co-operative; *
Boland Co-operative;
Perdeberg Co-operative;
Windmeul Co-operative;
Simonsvlei Co-operative;
Drakenstein Co-operative;
Franschhoek Co-operative.
* Wines are not sold at these co-operative cellars.

The estates **Welgemeend** and **Le Bonheur** also fall within the Paarl district.

UNION WINE

Union Wine, the fourth biggest liquor concern in South Africa, has its headquarters in Wellington near Paarl. It was established in 1947 as the Union Wine and Spirit Corporation, later becoming part of the Picbel group.

In 1970 the company took over production on the **Bellingham** estate, which had originally been settled by a Huguenot named De Villiers, but by the 1940's production had dwindled to almost nothing. The estate was then bought by a retired S.A.A.F. captain, Bernard Podlashuk, who revived wine production on the estate while his wife restored the manor house.

The estate also produces lemons, plums and peaches, but under the direction of Union Wine the emphasis is on modernised cellar facilities and increased wine production.

The estate is not open to the public, but Bellingham wines are available through major outlets, along with other Union Wine products, such as Culemborg and Val du Charron wines, and Black and White Scotch whisky.

TULBAGH

You cannot rush through this remarkable village; it takes time to savour one of the country's most tranquil streets, which has been declared a national monument in its entirety. When Church Street with its neat row of white-washed, thatched cottages was restored after the shattering earthquake which rocked Tulbagh in 1969, restorers were able to reconstruct the buildings in their original mould and give the village back more than the earthquake had taken. One of these buildings, below and on the river side of Church Street, is a long, low structure known as Paddagang. After its restoration it was turned into the first KWV Wine House and today still draws people from near and far. The meals are splendid, as are the wines from the area, served in a peaceful and gracious surrounding.

The three estates situated in this district produce wines that are recognised for quality and

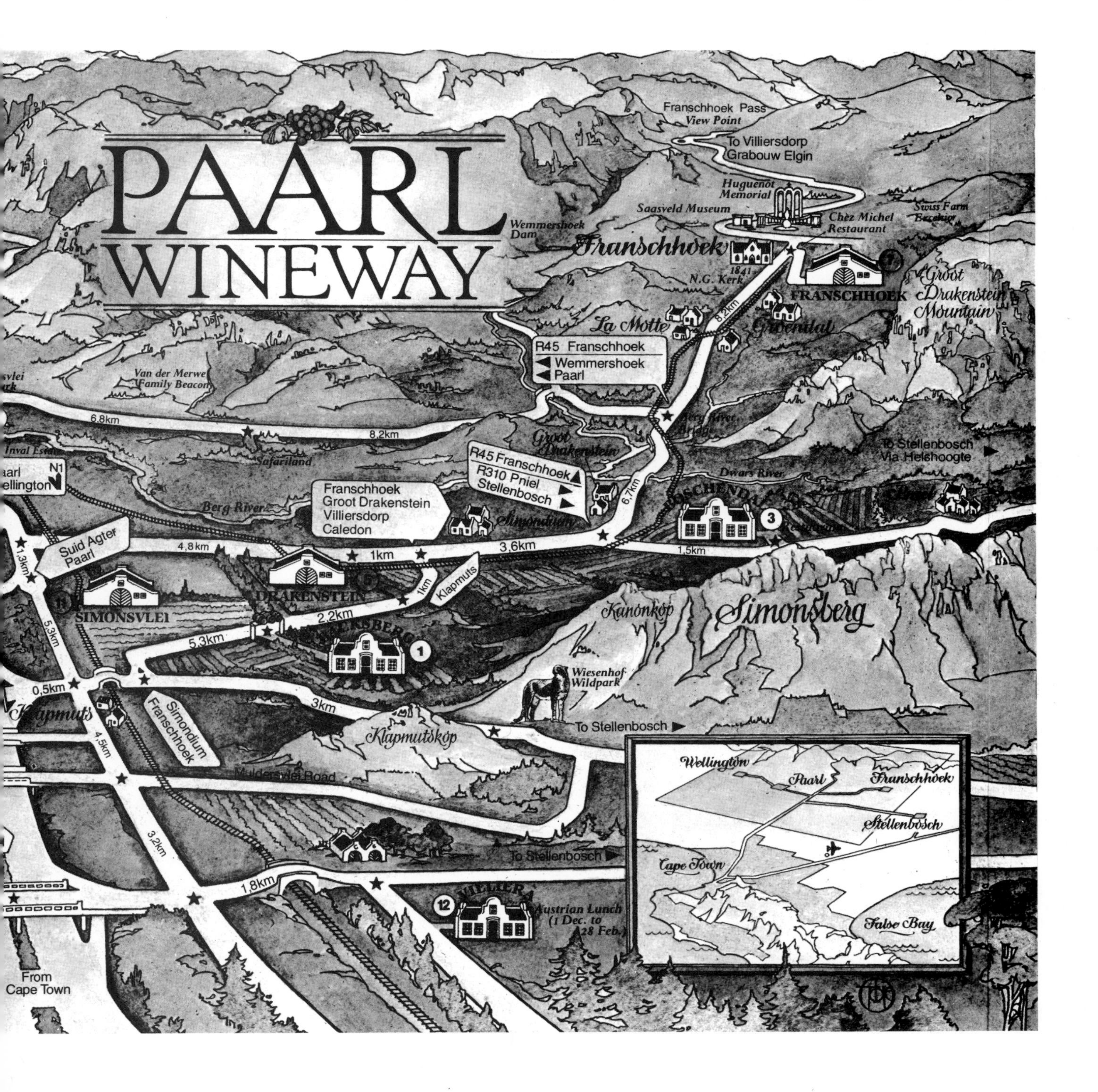

consistency. At **Twee Jonge Gezellen** estate N.C. Krone and his son Nicky are dedicated producers and lovers who have produced prestigious wines for many years. N.C. Krone is without any doubt one of our leading and most popular wine-makers, and his son is showing the same calibre. Although good red wines are produced on the estate, the name is more often connected with delicate, well-balanced whites. These wines are not for sale on the estate and visits are by appointment only.

Equally well-known are the wines and people of **Montpellier** near Tulbagh. Mr De Wet Theron has developed the estate into a prime example of wine-farming excellence. Among the superb white wines made on the estate is the special riesling produced from grapes grown in the "garden vine-yard" — grapes that have been pampered to produce a wine with an individual character.

Wine is sold on the estate, but please 'phone before setting out to Montpellier. Tel: 02362-3904.

Another extremely popular name amongst lovers of good white wines is **Theuniskraal.** The wine is produced on the Theuniskraal estate near Tulbagh by Kobus Jordaan but bottled and marketed through the Bergkelder. Kobus' father set the tradition of sound wines from Theunis-kraal many years ago and today there is still something of the peace and goodliness of the Tulbagh valley in these wines.

The estate can only be visited by appointment.

The Drostdy Co-operative, the oldest co-op in South Africa, is also situated in Tulbagh.

While in this area a visit can be made to Wolseley where the Romans River Co-operative Wine Cellar is situated, and across Michell's Pass further on to the picturesque town of Ceres.

This beautiful valley, known as the Land of Waveren, is surrounded by blue mountain ranges, covered with vineyards and inhabited by hos-pitable people. It is a valley with its own heart-beat, one that should never change, and a haven the visitor always returns to.

BREEDE RIVER VALLEY

From Cape Town the long stretch of the Breede River Valley can be reached by travelling over either the Bains Kloof or the Du Toits Kloof Pass. Both routes offer the splendour of mountain ranges and a dramatic first glimpse of the valley. Mainly known as a region producing white wines of top quality, producers have proved that red wines from this area also deserve recognition. One thinks, for example, of the superb shiraz wines produced at the **Zandvliet** estate (near Ashton — wines not sold to the public) by Paul de Wet and his son. The following estates can be visited and sell wine:

Bergsig estate is situated at the foot of the Bains Kloof Pass alongside the Breede and White Rivers. White, red and dessert wines are sold and visits can be made by appointment. Tel: 02324-603.

In the Slanghoek Valley, about 5 km from Rawsonville, the traveller will come across the oldest farm in the valley, **Opstal** estate. The present owner is in the fifth generation continuing a wine-making tradition. Only dry and semi-sweet white and dessert wines are pro-duced. Tel: 0231-91066.

Also in the Rawsonville district and 5 km from the Goudini Spa, **Lebensraum** estate has been farmed by the Deetlefs family since 1822. Dry and semi-sweet as well as dessert wines are sold on the estate, but sales hours are limited.
Tel: 0231-91137.

Excelsior estate is situated near Ashton and owned by the De Wet family. Wine-production here is centred around full-bodied sweet fortified wines, which can be bought by the public.
Tel: 023422-2212, 2222.

Before entering Bonnievale, where excellent cheeses are made, the vineyards of the **Welte-vrede** estate will most definitely attract the atten-tion. This flourishing estate belongs to the enter-prising young wine-maker, Lourens Jonker.

Weltevrede was the first estate in the Breede River Valley to market wines directly to the public and today a wide range of high quality wines can be sampled and bought here. Tours of the cellars can also be arranged. Tel: 023432-2730.

Estates that do not sell wine to the public include:

Mont Blois (near Robertson), **Rietvallei** (between Robertson and Ashton), **Zandvliet** (but don't leave the Cape without tasting this estate's shiraz), **De Wetshof** (on the road from Robertson to Bonnievale and another well-known wine name) and **Goedverwacht** (outside Bonnievale).

The following co-operative wine-cellars are situated in the Breede River Valley and are mentioned as they are situated from near Wolseley to the Swellendam district and as far afield as Villiersdorp:
Aan-de-Doorns;
Agterkliphoogte;
Ashton;
Aufwaerts;
Badsberg;
Bonnievale;
Botha;
Brandvlei;
Clairvaux;
Dutoitskloof;
Goudini;
Grooteiland;
Langverwacht;
Lateganskop; *
Louwshoek-Voorsorg;
McGregor;
Merwespont;
Merwida;
Nordale;

Nuwehoop;
Nuy;
Overhex;
Robertson;
Romansrivier;
Rooiberg;
Slanghoek;
Stettyn;
Waboomsrivier

* Wine not for sale.

Most of these co-operative cellars have produced extremely popular wines of sound quality. The names of Merwida, Rooiberg, Nuy, Roodezandt, Robertson and Botha will not be unfamiliar and in spite of the large number of these wine-cellars in the region, the discriminating wine investigator will find it well worth while visiting these progressive co-operatives.

LITTLE KAROO

The Little Karoo district is a long, narrow stretch of land with much charm. Starting at Montagu in the west it carries on through Barrydale, Ladismith, Calitzdorp and Oudtshoorn to De Rust.

The rainfall is fairly low (an average of 300 mm per annum) which makes irrigation necessary and suits cultivars such as palomino, muscat d' Alexandrie, cinsaut, chenin blanc and muscadel. The area is therefore known for its rebate and muscadel wines of very good quality. In recent years, however, the quality of table wines from the Little Karoo has shown tremendous improvement.

The area has one demarcated estate, **Die Krans** at Calitzdorp, where amongst others a highly regarded tinta barocca is produced.

Other attractions of the region include the charming town of Montagu with its warm spring baths, and Oudtshoorn, the home of ostriches and the impressive Cango Caves.

SWARTLAND

The Swartland wine district, which comprises the viticultural areas within the divisional boundaries of Malmesbury, stretches from north of Durbanville and Paarl and covers the area west of the Berg River to the Atlantic ocean. The undulating landscape is largely covered with wheat and as a wine-producing area it is comparatively new. In the past decade, however, a large variety of cultivars have been propagated with success.

Not far from Riebeeck West on the Kasteelberg slopes lies **Allesverloren** estate, granted in 1704. In 1872 the farm was bought by Daniel Francois Malan, father of the later Prime Minister Dr D.F. Malan, who was born on Allesverloren.

Wine was first made by a Malan, also christened Daniel Francois, who realised the potential for port wines in his area many years ago. The port wines of Allesverloren are still regarded with reverence, but under the supervision of the present owner, S.F. (Fanie) Malan, the estate's range of wines has been expanded to include cabernet sauvignon, pinotage, cinsaut, shiraz and tinta barocca. Marketing of these wines is done through the Bergkelder.

The majority of wine-farmers deliver their harvest to the following co-operatives: Mamreweg, Swartland and Riebeeck Wine Farmers.

PIQUETBERG DISTRICT

Stretching from the mountains to the Atlantic Ocean, the district is fairly flat except around the town of Piquetberg.

Dry white wines, dessert wines, rebate and distilling wines are produced here and only one farmer makes his own wine — the rest deliver to the Porterville Co-operative.

OLIFANTS RIVER REGION

The road through the Swartland and past Piquetberg eventually brings one to the Piekenierskloof Pass from the summit of which the Olifants River Valley unfolds, a soft valley surrounded by mountains and stretching along the meandering Olifants River. It is a graceful landscape, green against magnificent cliffs, ravines and valleys. This is a fertile valley of citrus and other deciduous fruits as well as bush tea (rooibostee) but the table wines of the area should not be underestimated. Starting at Citrusdal the region stretches northwards to Klawer, Trawal, Vredendal and Lutzville — an ever-changing landscape.

Most of the grapes in the region are delivered to the following co-operatives, which are fine examples of dedication and innovation: Citrusdal, Trawal, Klawer, Spruitdrift, Lutzville and Olifantsrivier. The Citrusdal production cellar sells all its wines in bottles, while the three largest co-ops operating as a single unit in the country are Olifantsrivier, Lutzville and Klawer.

No one passing through this region should be in a hurry. The Cedarberg is a haven that has to be explored, and this can be done while following a wine trail. Turning right at the Algeria signpost the road leads steeply and windingly to unspoilt beauty — and also the single wine-maker on the summit of the mountain. Oom Pollie Niewoudt, as he is lovingly known, has farmed on Dwarsrivier for a lifetime. It was only in the seventies that he turned his hand to wine-making and not only did he succeed in achieving what others thought was impossible, but with his first entry in the regional wine show he was proclaimed champion wine-maker in the region.

In this vicinity stop-overs can be made at the

camping site at Algeria or huts rented from private farmers. Inquiries to the Town Clerk of Clanwilliam.

In spring the region is carpeted with wild flowers. Other places not to be missed are the Bidou Valley, the Wupperthal Mission Station and the Ramskop Nature Reserve. The Pakhuis Pass leads to the grave of Louis Leipoldt, Afrikaans poet, child of this earth, wine-lover and connoisseur and writer of cookery books that are today still used as reference when traditional dishes are discussed.

LOWER ORANGE RIVER REGION

What remains for the traveller to discover, is the district located on both banks of the Orange River from Groblershoop to the Augrabies Falls. Alluvial and fertile soil where the river branches to create islands, as well as on the river banks, have been proved well suited to the propagation of vineyards. Even further from the river the gravelly Karoo soils are producing reasonably well. All vineyards are irrigated. It is a kindly river to travel along, with hospitable people and old-world charm. The most important cultivar planted here is sultana, followed by muscat d' Alexandrie. Much of this output is destined for the production of raisins. Colombar and chenin blanc have also been planted with success.

The bulk of wine-production is destined for brandy and wine-spirit, but table wines are also produced. The grapes are delivered to the Orange River Wine Cellars which has five independently operating wineries at Upington, Grootdrink, Keimoes, Kakamas and Groblershoop.

Exploring the wine route from Cape Town northwards, one discovers estate after beautiful estate, each one with homestead, cellar and vineyards. These perfect microcosms are like the cells of a living organism, following separately but in unison the rhythm of the seasons, a cycle into which are bound the lives and efforts of the gentle but dedicated wine-makers. Gradually one perceives how the essential spirit of the winelands springs inseparably from good earth, good wine and good people.

LIST OF DEMARCATED DISTRICTS FOR WINE ESTATES

ESTATE	DISTRICT	ESTATE	DISTRICT
Allesverloren	Swartland	Meerendal	Durbanville
Alto	Stellenbosch	Meerlust	Stellenbosch
Audacia	Stellenbosch	Middelvlei	Stellenbosch
Backsberg	Paarl	Mooiplaas	Stellenbosch
Bergsig	Worcester	Montagne	Stellenbosch
Bonfoi	Stellenbosch	Mont Blois	Robertson
Boschendal	Paarl	Montpellier	Tulbagh
Devonvale Estate	Stellenbosch	Muratie	Stellenbosch
De Wetshof	Robertson	Neethlingshof	Stellenbosch
De Zoete Inval	Paarl	Opstal	Worcester
Die Krans	Little Karoo	Overgaauw	Stellenbosch
Diemersdal	Durbanville	Rietvallei	Robertson
Excelsior	Robertson	Rust-en-Vrede	Stellenbosch
Fairview	Paarl	Schoongezicht	Stellenbosch
Goede Hoop	Stellenbosch	Simonsig	Stellenbosch
Goedverwacht	Robertson	Spier	Stellenbosch
Groot Constantia	Constantia	Theuniskraal	Tulbagh
Hazendal	Stellenbosch	Twee Jonge Gezellen	Tulbagh
Jacobsdal	Stellenbosch	Uiterwyk	Stellenbosch
Johann Graue	Paarl	Uitkyk	Stellenbosch
Kanonkop	Stellenbosch	Verdun	Stellenbosch
Koopmanskloof	Stellenbosch	Vergenoegd	Stellenbosch
Laborie	Paarl	Villiera	Paarl
Landskroon	Paarl	Vredenheim	Stellenbosch
Lebensraum	Worcester	Welgemeend	Paarl
Le Bonheur	Paarl/Stellenbosch	Weltevrede	Robertson
		Zandvliet	Robertson

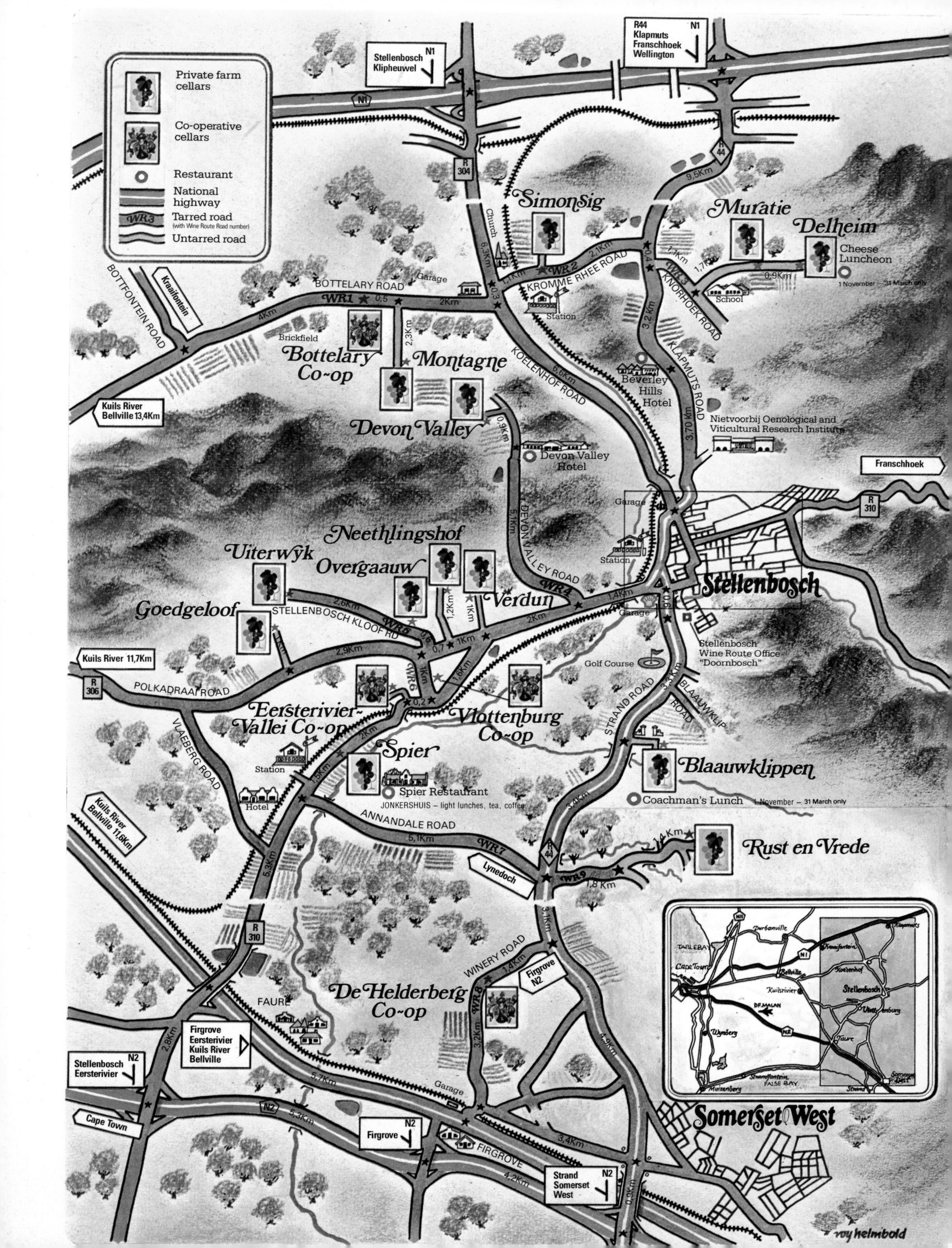

Private farm cellars
Co-operative cellars
Restaurant
National highway
Tarred road (with Wine Route Road number)
Untarred road
Stellenbosch Klipheuwel
R44 Klapmuts Franschhoek Wellington
Simonsig
Muratie
Delheim
Cheese Luncheon
1 November – 31 March only
KROMME RHEE ROAD
KNORHOEK ROAD
BOTTELARY ROAD
BOTTFONTEIN ROAD
Kraaifontein
Bottelary Co-op
Brickfield
Montagne
Devon Valley
Devon Valley Hotel
KOELENHOF ROAD
Beverley Hills Hotel
KLAPMUTS ROAD
Nietvoorbij Oenological and Viticultural Research Institute
Franschhoek
Kuils River Bellville 13,4Km
Neethlingshof
Uiterwyk
Overgaauw
Verdun
Goedgeloof
DEVON VALLEY ROAD
STELLENBOSCH KLOOF RD
Stellenbosch
Station
Garage
Stellenbosch Wine Route Office "Doornbosch"
Golf Course
Kuils River 11,7Km
POLKADRAAI ROAD
Eersterivier-Vallei Co-op
Vlottenburg Co-op
STRAND ROAD
BLAAUWKLIP ROAD
Blaauwklippen
Coachman's Lunch
1 November – 31 March only
Spier
Spier Restaurant
JONKERSHUIS – light lunches, tea, coffee
VLAEBERG ROAD
Hotel
Kuils River Bellville 11,6Km
ANNANDALE ROAD
Rust en Vrede
Lynedoch
WINERY ROAD
De Helderberg Co-op
Firgrove N2
FAURE
Firgrove Eersterivier Kuils River Bellville
Stellenbosch Eersterivier
Cape Town
Firgrove
FIRGROVE
Strand Somerset West
Somerset West
TABLEBAY
Durbanville
Cape Town
Bellville
Kuilsrivier
Koelenhof
Klapmuts
Kraaifontein
Stellenbosch
Vlottenburg
DF MALAN
Wynberg
Faure
Strandfontein
FALSE BAY
Muizenberg
Strand
Somerset West
roy helmbold

2

3

1 Previous page: Winter winelands at *Meerendal* in Durbanville.
2 From the arched doorway of the historic wine cellar at *Groot Constantia* one looks onto the homestead, and the careful alignment of the buildings creates a sense of ordered harmony.
3 Famous old Constantia wine bottles which are now housed in the Stellenryck Wine Museum, Stellenbosch.
4 Golden evening light slants through the *Groot Constantia* kitchen, highlighting the polish of years on copper, brass and old red tiles.

4

5

5 The *Groot Constantia* manor house.
6 Autumn colours on the slopes of the *Groot Constantia* estate.

6

7

7 Cape vineyards between Stellenbosch and Paarl.

8

9

10

8 Interior of the *Volkskombuis,* Stellenbosch. Old Cape cooking is combined with a fine selection of the wines of the region in this popular restaurant.
9 Many of the buildings on Dorp Street, Stellenbosch, have been declared national monuments.
10 Brandy maturation cellar of the Oudemeester group, at Stellenbosch.

11

12

11 Old Dutch wall tiles at *De Oude Molen,* head office of Gilbeys at Stellenbosch, installed by René Santhagen, pioneer of South African brandy.
12 Harvest.
13 *Schoongezicht,* Stellenbosch, is known for its wine and also for its herd of Jersey cows.
14-16 Overleaf: Bottle maturation cellar and tasting room at *Die Bergkelder,* where cellar tours are conducted twice daily.

15

16

17

18

17 Grapes being brought to the cellar at *Neethlingshof,* Stellenbosch.
18 The emblem of René Santhagen. The motto 'Always on target' refers to the old custom of shooting at the *papegaai* (popinjay), a parrot-shaped target.
19 The annual Van der Stel Birthday celebrations in Stellenbosch.

19

20

20 Devon Valley, near Stellenbosch.

21

24

21 Interior of the Stellenryck Wine Museum.
22 Wood-carving on an old wine wagon in the museum.
23 The Stellenryck Wine Museum is housed in a building which used to be the wine cellar of a homestead dating back to the 18th century. The prominent Krige family (Issie Krige married General Jan Smuts) once owned this estate.
24 Vat with carved head in the *Bergkelder* cellar depicting the three ships which arrived at the Cape in 1652 under the command of Jan van Riebeeck.

22

23

DROMMEDARIS – GOEDE HOOP – REYGER
6 APRIL 1652

25

26

25 *Blaauwklippen,* where cellar tours are conducted during the season, and apart from wine there is a variety of pickles and wine *worst* on sale.
26 Una van der Spuy's house, *Old Nectar,* on the way to Jonkershoek.
27 The cellar of *Rust en Vrede,* owned by the famous rugby Springbok, Jannie Engelbrecht.
28 A full-costume pageant forms part of the annual Van der Stel Birthday celebrations.

27

28

29

29 The *Boschendal* manor house, from the vineyards.
30 The door-knocker of *Hazendal* estate.
31 The restaurant at *Boschendal* in the original wine cellar which probably dates back to before 1800.
32 Old farm wall at *Hazendal*.
33 Overleaf: Wild mustard covering the wineland in winter in the Klapmuts area.

30

31

34 Summer landscape at Banhoek.

34

35 Autumn landscape at Banhoek.

35

36 This gable at *Groenhof* farm is one of the oldest and most beautiful on the wine route.
37 Cognac still in the Distillers Brandy Museum, Stellenbosch. This building was orginally designed by Sir Herbert Baker for the Rhodes Fruit Farms.
38 Summer vineyards in Stellenbosch.
39 *Die Kruithuis,* the old powder magazine on the *Braak* (common) in Stellenbosch, now houses a military museum.

36

39

37

38

40

41

40 Pressing season at *Muratie*.
41 The *Muratie* façade.

42

42 Ben Prins, winemaker of *Muratie,* who still utilises "spontaneous fermentation" in his delightful cellar.
43 Annemarie Canitz, the owner of *Muratie,* in her drawing room.

43

44

45

44 *Spier* estate, Lynedoch: the manor house, which is beautifully restored.
45 The gable of the old slave quarters at *Spier*.

46 The restaurant at *Spier*.
47 The 18th century dovecote at *Meerlust*, one of two still in existence.

46

48

49

50

51

48 Installing large maturation vats in the *Meerlust* cellar.
49, 50 Farmhands at *Meerlust*.
51 Georgio Dalla Sia, *Meerlust* wine-maker, checking his harvest.

52 Previous page: A farm dwarfed by the mountains near Worcester.
53-55 Exterior and details of *Uitkyk*, between Stellenbosch and Paarl.

58

59

60

56 Wine cellar on the farm *Het Verblyf der Gelukzaligen* ('The dwelling-place of those who have been blessed').
57 Vineyards in spring at *Middelvlei,* on the outskirts of Stellenbosch.
58-61 An annual cutting auction, reflecting the moods and anxieties of the traders.

61

62 The back yard of *Vergenoegd,* at Faure.
63 Oak vats with carved heads such as these in the *Delheim* cellar are cherished as heirlooms.
64 Franschhoek.
65 Overleaf: Autumn vineyards in Paarl.

63

64

66

67

68

66 Looking down from the stables at *Die Nuwe Plantasie,* Paarl.
67 Gunther Brözel, *Nederburg* winemaker, in his red wine maturation cellar.
68 The annual international auction of Cape wines is held at *Nederburg*.
69 The *Nederburg* homestead.

69

70

71

72

70 Winetasting at the annual show of young wines at Paarl.
71 Coopers plying their trade at a cooperage in Paarl.
72 The opening of *Laborie,* one of the KWV wine houses, which took the form of an evening garden party, in front of the manor house.
73 Another house in the *Laborie* complex.
74 *Laborie* façade in summer.

73

74

75

76

75 The famous Paarl Valley in the heart of the winelands.
76 An old door with a grape motif at the estate *Allesverloren,* well known for its port, in Riebeek West.

77

78

79

80

77 A vineyard in the Riebeek West area.
78 *Paddagang,* Tulbagh, one of several wine houses of the KWV which serve as restaurants where food and wine of the region can be enjoyed.
79 The Drostdy sherry maturation cellar at Tulbagh.
80 Church Street in Tulbagh, the whole of which is a national monument. It was restored after serious damage was caused by earth tremors in 1969.
81 Overleaf: Landscape in the Swartland district near Malmesbury.

83

82, 83 Harvest.
84 Mountains in the winelands near Worcester.
85 Overleaf: Contour-ploughed vineyards in the Paarl area.

84

36
37

90

92

90 Winter ploughing at Goudini, near Worcester.
91 The Hex River Valley, where grapes are grown for the table.
92 Concentration is needed to avoid bruising the bunches intended for table grapes.

94

93 The Koo Valley, between Touws River and Montagu.
94 Pruning in the Klein Karoo.

93

95

96

95 Remote dwelling on the outskirts of the Robertson winelands.
96 Harvesting the noble Cabernet.
97 Overleaf: A co-operative wine cellar at Bonnievale.

100

101

98 Previous page, left: In the Robertson district the mountains are overwhelming.
99 Previous page, right: Ploughing in the McGregor area.
100-102 After the pressing season, usually March-April, the town of Montagu hosts the annual Muscadel Festival, which officially lasts two days but, for some, much longer!

102

103

104

105

106

103 Deserted farmhouse in the Robertson district.
104 *Mont Blois* estate nestles in the shelter of the Langeberg mountain range.
105, 106 Winelands people.

107

108

109

107 A farmer of the old stamp, in a remote area of the winelands near Oudtshoorn, with his old-fashioned brandy still.
108, 109 Labourers at harvesting time.
110 Landscape near Villiersdorp.
111 Overleaf: Sunrise over the mountains near Montagu.

110